# In Conversation With…Small Press Publishers

*Edited by Isabelle Kenyon and Dr. Charley Barnes*

First published April 2021 by Fly on the Wall Press

Published in the UK by

Fly on the Wall Press

56 High Lea Rd

New Mills

Derbyshire

SK22 3DP


www.flyonthewallpress.co.uk


ISBN: 978-1-913211-53-0

Copyright Isabelle Kenyon and Charley Barnes © 2021


The right of Isabelle Kenyon and Charley Barnes to be identified as the editors of this work has been asserted in accordance with the Copyright, Designs and Patents Act 1988.


Typesetting and Cover Design by Isabelle Kenyon.

# Editor's Letter – *by Charley Barnes and Isabelle Kenyon*

I was delighted when Charley approached me about the prospect of collating all UK small presses into a book. The hopes were that this would be an invaluable guide for individuals with a manuscript searching for a home for their work. We wanted this to be a personal book for individuals who find the publishing industry inaccessible. Often, when writers complete the manuscript, whether alone, or as part of a course or degree, they go straight to the UK's largest publishing houses, and due to the competitive nature of these publishing companies, most will not have the success they desire when querying here.

Small publishers, we believe, shape the UK industry by offering diverse and exciting texts from underrepresented authors. Often, small publishers experiment with cross genre works and are able to move faster than large publishing houses may be able to, whether this is due to an absence of bureaucracy or simply shorter production lines!

In conversation with Charley, we discussed how we wanted this book to be presented and we considered the excellent guides which are out there already for writers. Therefore, we didn't want this to be another guide on a bookshelf, but a personalised experience of curated small publishers from across the UK whom we feel cater for all genres of manuscripts, and who each offer something unique to the writing community.

Here you will get a sense for the personalities of small publishers which I felt was important for us to communicate, as of course, small publishers tend to work on a much smaller scale. After manuscript acceptance, writers will work in close proximity with the editors, cover designers and potentially marketing teams! Charley and I hope this will both be an interesting read for you and that the journey of reading may end in a successful manuscript query for you. **– Isabelle Kenyon**

When Isabelle and I opened a dialogue around the possibility of this book, we knew that we needed something distinct as well as helpful. There are already several reputable guides to publishing, and indeed smaller press work, available on the market. However, there wasn't, we felt, one that offered a more personal touch; a sit-down with an editor, to get to the meat of the matter. We decided, then, an interview format where we went straight to the heart of it all — the submission process, the preferred genre, the contract details — would make life easier for writers and editors alike.

Isabelle and I are no strangers to the submission process, namely because we've both worked with small presses in the UK and had hugely positive experiences with them (not to forget the fact, of course, that Isabelle runs her own successful press as well). So, between us we considered the things we, as authors, would like to know more about, and the presses who submitted to this project were kind and transparent enough to answer us — which is exactly what the publishing industry needs more of!

After years of working with Creative Writing students, I thought — as did Isabelle — it was worth putting something together to showcase opportunities away from big name publishers. This is exactly what we've looked to achieve through In Conversations with... A guide for people looking where to start; whether that's for the first ever submission or whether it's for something new that you're looking for a fresh home for. Whatever the manuscript, we hope that there will be a publisher in this collection to cater to your writing needs. — **Charley Barnes**

# Contents

# Shopping around for the right home

"Ultimately, you must work with people you feel comfortable with."

Finding the right publisher for a manuscript is like finding the right partner: When you know, you know. There is, however, a misnomer among young writers — or rather, aspiring writers — that any offer is a good offer. That isn't to say that a press will misrepresent your work, or not do their best insofar as editing and marketing, and all the other avenues that lead to book release. A press's best interests, though, may not always be the right fit. It's no one's fault, necessarily, but it's worth keeping this in mind before you settle down with any publisher — whether they be big or niche.

Ultimately, you must work with people you feel comfortable with. In my own writing background, I once had an offer made on my first novel and, after I'd finished cheering with delight, I realised something didn't feel quite right about it. The press was new, but so was I — so what did that matter? The editors were two authors who I happened to admire, having read their work and various interviews with them, so I trusted that my writing would be safe. Still, something didn't feel how I imagined it might — the joy of finally having found a home for a work! Even though I couldn't put my finger on what was wrong, exactly, I opted for clarity with the editors to explain that even though I was delighted, I also wasn't ready. They kindly replied to tell me the offer was open-ended, and that if I wanted to shop around I was certainly free to — but going back to them was an option, too.

I don't suppose all editors would be quite so accommodating. However, after further searching, I found a bigger firm — with a marketing team, too — who made an offer on the book, and I've placed a further five manuscripts with this publisher since. The moral of this story, then, is that you aren't obliged to take the first offer that comes along. You *are* allowed to have faith that your work will find a bigger home, or a more experimental home or... whatever home it needs! You are allowed to say 'No' to offers.
— **Charley**

*In Conversation with... Camilla Reeve*

*How should a writer with a manuscript approach your press?*
An increasing proportion of our books are written by or about refugees or by authors from other marginalised groups. If you're writing on subjects related to Human Rights, Refugees, Justice, Equality, the Environment, Climate Change or Sustainability and would like to submit your work for possible publication after December 2021, please check our submission guidelines at https://palewellpress.co.uk/Submission-Guide-lines.html

*What does a standard author contract look like for you?*
We retain exclusive rights for 20 years to publish the book in English. Authors get 10 free copies, can buy more at a discount, and receive royalties on all other copies sold. Royalties are paid in July for books sold up to the preceding March. We don't pay advances. Authors can also ask us to produce an eBook and, if they have access to free recording facilities, an audiobook.

*What styles are you looking for? Are you open to cross-genre submissions?*
We publish long and short fiction, non-fiction and poetry. Books may include more than one genre, e.g. poetry and narratives. We don't publish humorous writing, plays, or books for young children but we have some YA works in the pipeline.

*How do you judge the success of a book?*
A successful Palewell Press book looks beautiful, makes the author happy and represents what he or she really believes. It should foster Justice, Equality and Sustainability. It may not sell more than a few hundred copies but it gives voice to views that might otherwise be suppressed or ignored.

Its message and the empowerment generated in the author's community can change lives.

*What's your favourite ever book?*
"The Left-Hand of Darkness" by Ursula Le Guin.

*How are authors expected to support marketing for their book?*
Authors work alongside Palewell Press using social media and email to market their work. One or more readings are arranged by Palewell Press. Poetry films or audio samples made by the author are useful in generating interest. Authors can suggest people to write the blurb or to review the finished book. It's great if they can persuade the owner of a local bookshop to stock their book, or they know someone organising a book festival.

*We asked Palewell Press to select titles which represented their work...*

### Testimony of Flight
By Jane Spiro

Jane Spiro's extraordinary collection of poetry and narrative - tells stories of forced migration and the consequences which impact years later. The book brings together historical moments and stories from members of Jane's family, starting with her father who left Poland as a 16-year-old on Kristallnacht. The content is further illuminated through years of conversations with other migrants and survivors from zones of strife, famine, revolution and war.

**"Can you hear the people sing?"**
A Palewell Press anthology.

A global set of writers share pandemic
experiences - lockdown, losing track
of time, a reprieve for nature - and
their hopes: from Yan Li on suffering
in China, through Joseph Kaifala in
Sierra Leone; Iranian-born Sholeh
Wolpé, María Cristina Azcona in
Argentina, and Simon Lichman in
Israel, to UK-based human rights
advocates like Nasrin Parvaz and
Shanta Acharya plus other wonderful
writers.

*Contact details*
Submissions and correspondence to enquiries@palewellpress.co.uk

Online bookstore is available at: https://palewellpress.co.uk
Social media channels are: https://twitter.com/PalewellPress
https://facebook.com/palewellpress

# POINT POSITIVE PRESS

*How should a writer with a manuscript approach your press?*
A writer should approach us with a finished manuscript that meets our ethos and an open mind by submitting to our email pointpositivepublishing@ gmail.com. We are happy to help with formatting and editing, as well as creating innovative projects that want to leap off the page and be something more.

*What does a standard author contract look like for you?*
Currently we are only publishing collaborative work and anthologies so we accept work with no fee and offer a free copy of the anthology to the authors included. Authors retain all rights to their work but we ask that they credit us as a publication. In 2021 we will be expanding into accepting individual work and publishing authors through our press.

*What styles are you looking for? Are you open to cross-genre submissions?*
We are open to cross-genre submissions and welcome them. We like to create books that are a little different, that maybe can't find a specific genre or a home within traditional media and publishers. We like our books to have depth and a bit of grit to them.

*Contact details:*
**Email:** pointpositivepublishing@gmail.com

# Submission guidelines and being respectful of them

"They need to know you're an author who can represent yourself and be respectful of others in the industry."

It may seem like an obvious piece of advice, but adhering to submissions guidelines should be high up on your list of priorities when you look to submit work. Why? Because editors, agents and publishers are people, too! They're working hard to represent a whole family of book publications – sometimes single-handedly– and paying close attention to the submission guidelines can be the first step to get you through the door.

**Consider things like:**

- Have I checked and double-checked this publisher is accepting manuscripts?
- Do I know my work, in terms of genre and content (for example), is something they might be interested in?
- Have I checked the publisher's name, so I can politely address this submission?

If you're looking to place your work with someone who will take care of it, they also need to know you're an author who can represent yourself and be respectful of others in the industry. It *can* be difficult to navigate these guidelines sometimes, especially given that there is no standardised format for them. This ultimately means each press will have their own set of rules. Pay close attention, though, because it's a good investment of your time. **– Charley**

*How should a writer with a manuscript approach your press?*
The first step in approaching us is to check out the submissions page on our website, that way you'll discover when our reading windows are open. If you contact us by email, please show you've done your research on us by using our names, and letting us know why you think we might be a good fit for your work. Alternatively, you might come across us at a book fair, and we can chat in person.

*What does a standard author contract look like for you?*
Contracts define the relationship between publisher and author. Including definition of the work, delivery of the manuscript, editing, proofreading, and rights granted to the publisher. We agree to format, distribute and price the work and we explain the publication timescale. Copyright, royalty payments and third-party permissions are covered, as well as all other rights. We state the number of author copies that will be available, our publicity and marketing strategies, and the procedure for reversion and termination of contract.

*What styles are you looking for? Are you open to cross-genre submissions?*
We publish poetry and long-form fiction. We look for writing with an immersive sense of place, strong characterisation and subtle lyricism. We tend not to look for genres in our fiction, because for us it's much more about the situation and feeling of a book. In poetry we prefer a more narrative style than wildly experimental.

We hand make our own pamphlets, and publish these throughout the year along with a small selection of novels, novellas and full poetry collections.

*How do you judge the success of a book?*

We publish books whose authors would have to wait a long time, if not forever, to find an agent prepared to risk trying to sell their work to a commercial publisher. Our books are unique. We know this from the feedback we get from book bloggers and other readers who let us know their thoughts. Their emotional reactions. How beautiful they found the book as a physical object. How it's stayed with them. That's our measure of success.

*What's your favourite ever book?*

This changes according to mood, memory, and whatever I might have read since. On this occasion I'm going to answer '*Once Upon a River*' by Diane Setterfield (December 2018). The setting of the River Thames in 1887 is threaded through with superstition and folklore. It's a deeply immersive story of multiple characters, landscape, sorrow, and human spirit. Much older but somehow along similar lines, I'll mention Thomas Hardy's '*Tess of the d'Urbervilles*' which stayed with me in the same way.

*How are authors expected to support marketing for their book?*

As a tiny publisher we expect authors to work in partnership with us in employing whatever marketing strategies they have available to help us promote their book. Largely social media, word of mouth and visiting independent bookshops where possible. At the outset, we engage a social media tour operator to organise an online cover reveal and a blog tour in which the author and their book are featured on multiple book blogs over the course of a week.

*We asked Wild Pressed Books to select a title which represented their work...*

**Bella**
by R.M. Francis

A spectre has haunted Netherton for generations. Everyone has a theory, no one has an answer.

The woods that frame the housing estate uncover a series of heinous acts, drawing onlookers into a space of clandestine, queer sexuality: a liminal space of abject and uncanny experience.

A question echoes in the odd borderlands of being, of fear-fascination, attraction-repulsion, of sex and death.

Who put Bella down the Wych-Elm?

*Contact details*

Email: wildpressedbooks@gmail.com
Twitter: @wildpressed

*In Conversation with...Anne Holloway*

*How should a writer with a manuscript approach your press?*
Have a good read of our website and take a look at our publications, then contact us via email explaining why you want to be published, what your expectations are, and include a sample of your work.

*What does a standard author contract look like for you?*
We have no standard author contract, each contract is negotiated between us and the author depending on the amount of support required to progress a manuscript to publication. We call our model Peer Publishing and our authors own their books.

*What styles are you looking for? Are you open to cross-genre submissions?*
Although our focus has been predominantly poetry, we are open to all styles and welcome cross-genre submissions. To date we have published fiction, memoir, poetry, play scripts and non-fiction.

*Contact details:*
Anne Holloway at submissions@bigwhiteshed.co.uk

# *Online presence prior to publication*

*"If you have a strong online presence it will show an editor you are dedicated to building a brand."*

There is a horrible idea floating around out there that spending time on your social media profile, as a writer or artist, is somehow "time-wasting". Admittedly, there's a limit to how much time any one person can and/or should spend on social media platforms. If you're a writer who is actively promoting your work though, your best move is to consider this as simply part of the job.

The reason for upholding an online presence before publication is two-fold. On a practical level, it's important to remember that we live in a digital age and a publisher will likely search for you on social media when your name or your book becomes a serious buyable option for their Press. If you have a strong online presence it will show an editor you are dedicated to building a brand, engaging with (potential) readers, and putting work into your own marketing. Remember, too, that while some companies will partake in marketing for you, there's every chance a small press may not have the human-power. If they know they can count on you for reliable input, this makes you and your book a better product for a publisher to purchase.

The second reason, then, is that if you can reach out and make connections prior to publication, you will already have a reader base looking forward to your book coming out. This is a great start for any writer. A following doesn't have to mean likes by the thousand, but making meaningful connections (online) with other writers and readers will go a long way when it comes to your work getting its own engagement and reach.

You're a writer though, so when it comes to the point of feeling like an unpaid social media manager, you may need to address the way in which you balance your time. My advice to anyone looking to gain an online presence to promote themselves, or to ensure future promotion for their work, would be to pick one platform and get to know it. You can't manage them all at once. **– Charley**

## In Conversation with...Cherry Potts

*How should a writer with a manuscript approach your press?*
We have regular open calls for anthologies, both short story and poetry, sometimes both in the same book, so they should check our submissions page for open calls. Once we have published you in an anthology, we will invite you to submit a collection of stories or poems, or novel(la). We also invite submissions if we see work elsewhere that is a good fit. We don't read unsolicited MS.

*What does a standard author contract look like for you?*
We pay royalties 8% cover price on physical books, 25% net receipts on eBooks. Divided between all authors. For anthologies we ask for 1-2-year exclusivity, for a collection/novel 10 years. Authors get 1-2 free copies for anthologies, 10 for a collection/novel, and discount on further copies. We don't pay royalty until the book has covered its costs, but the royalty is accrued and accounts sent annually. Most books make costs within the first year.

*What styles are you looking for? Are you open to cross-genre submissions?*
We are open to most things apart from romance, erotica and horror. Non-fiction we would only commission. We love cross genre! Particularly fond of slipstream - anything with a fantastical edge, SF, magic realism... Humour is a very personal thing so something that is setting out to be funny first and foremost would be treated warily. We also publish books for older children (8+) in the same genres as our adult work.

*Contact details:*
Website: Arachnepress.com
Twitter and Instagram: @arachnepress

*In Conversation with…Sarah Leavesley*

*How should a writer with a manuscript approach your press?*
V. Press has submissions windows, with details on our website at https://vpresspoetry.blogspot.com/p/submissions.html. Outside of those, we do sometimes reply to polite enquiries about manuscript submissions from writers already known to V. Press.

*What does a standard author contract look like for you?*
V. Press contracts ask writers to confirm that the work isn't defamatory and is their own copyright. They cover a certain number of free copies. Royalties depend on the type of book. Our print titles also include writers not having another pamphlet or book out for 6 or 12 months following their V. Press title, so as to give the title chance to get some exposure and because of the amount of V. Press time that goes into each title. Our contract is quite simple compared to many.

*What styles are you looking for? Are you open to cross-genre submissions?*
V. Press editor Sarah Leavesley has wide-ranging tastes. The best way to get an idea of what V. Press publishes is to check out our website and try some of our titles. Strictly speaking, V. Press currently publishes poetry and flash fiction, including flash fiction novellas. But there are exceptions that prove the rule. We have some illustrated poetry pamphlets, collaborative pamphlets and a number of titles that could potentially have been labelled flash and/or prose poetry.

*Contact details:*
More information about V. Press can be found on the website: http://vpresspoetry.blogspot.co.uk/ or by following V. Press on Twitter @vpresspoetry. The email address is vpresspublishing@outook.com. V. Press is run by Sarah Leavesley.

*In Conversation with... Betsy Reavley*

*How should a writer with a manuscript approach your press?*
As an independent, digital focused publisher, we encourage writers to visit our website and follow our submissions guidelines.
In the first instance we require a cover letter, complete synopsis and a complete manuscript.
I would advise that knowing what a synopsis is and making sure it is the best it can be, puts the submitting author in the strongest possible position.
We happily consider unsolicited manuscripts.

*What does a standard author contract look like for you?*
Our contract focuses on being fair to both the author and publisher.
Since many of our authors are not represented by agents, our contract covers all areas from foreign, film and TV to audio rights.
We work hard in this area to arrange subleases which ensure the manuscript gets as much attention, through as many mediums as possible.

*What styles are you looking for? Are you open to cross-genre submissions?*
Bloodhound started off publishing crime and thrillers but in recent years we have broadened the range of genres we publish.
Ultimately, we focus on commercial fiction that will appeal to the eBook market.

*Contact details:*
Website: www.bloodhoundbooks.com
Email: submissions@bloodhoundbooks.com

*In Conversation with…Jessica Chandler*

*How should a writer with a manuscript approach your press?*
Please email your proposal to jess@prototypepublishing.co.uk, ensuring that all attachments are in PDF or Microsoft Word format.
Please include a general description and synopsis of the work, plus a sample. The sample should not exceed 20 pages; we will request the full manuscript if we are interested in reading more.
Please also include a brief biography and a list of any previously published work.

We would also like to know why you are interested in Prototype publishing your work, and recommend reading some of our past publications to confirm whether we are the right publisher for you.
We will aim to respond to your email within 3 months, and would be grateful if you could wait patiently for this time to pass.
We cannot offer detailed feedback if your submission is unsuccessful, but will endeavour to suggest alternative avenues for publication whenever we can.

*What does a standard author contract look like for you?*
Author contracts include a small advance payment, plus royalties paid once all production costs have been covered.

*What styles are you looking for? Are you open to cross-genre submissions?*
Prototype accepts submissions and proposals for works that fall into any of our four types: poetry, prose, interdisciplinary projects, and anthologies. We are interested in a wide range of work and encourage proposals which resist easy definition or categorisation. We want to publish work which is courageous, original, demanding and inquisitive. We like projects which require us to think of new forms and formats, and projects which might not easily find a home elsewhere.

We are particularly keen to receive submissions of debut novels or short story collections, interdisciplinary poetic projects and full-length poetry collections.

Submissions are open to all, regardless of age, gender, race, religion and background.

*Contact details*:
Email: jess@prototypepublishing.co.uk;
admin@prototypepublishing.co.uk
Website: https://prototypepublishing.co.uk/

# *A word on contracts*

"There is no such thing as a stupid question when it comes to contracts."

Before submitting to a publisher, it can be beneficial to discuss their typical author contract. I would do this by sending a polite email explaining that you are interested in sending a manuscript but would like to know what a typical author royalty rate may be, or if you will receive any author copies. Other useful things to ask are:

* Do you distribute worldwide?
* What formats would my book be available in?
* How many years do your contracts last for?
* Do you have existing relationships with bookshops?

These questions are purely to avoid any surprises later along the line! You are also within your rights to run a contract past an agent or a professional body such as the Society of Authors. Debut authors can sometimes shy away from asking detailed questions, but remember how much time and care you have put into writing your manuscript! You want to make sure your time and your skill is accounted for. Writing is a job like any other — it is my hope that author and publisher conversations about money will become more open and normalised. **— Isabelle**

There is nothing wrong with asking a publisher what their contract involves. In fact, it's a sensible thing to do. From experience, then, I've worked with some publishers who have been completely transparent about their contractual obligations to myself and my work — and, subsequently, my obligations to them — but I've also worked with some publishers without having a contract at all. That isn't to endorse that behaviour, necessarily, but more to raise it as a possibility when your work makes its way into the wild. I cannot stress enough, though, that these editors were people who I knew especially well and, despite not having a contract, I still knew exactly what was expected from both sides of the publishing agreement (albeit a verbal one).

There are things you should be asking, such as how the book is distributed and what relationship(s) the publisher has with bookshops. If you're placing with a new publisher though — and especially if you're placing a debut work — there is no such thing as a stupid question when it comes to contracts.

- Can I buy author copies? If so, what cost are they to me?
- Can I sell author copies, or should readers be directed to the publisher?
- And, the real biggie, what's your royalty breakdown?

There are some small publishers who won't pay a royalty at all, some who will provide a sample of author copies for free, some who want *everyone* to buy through them. You need to know these things to avoid surprises and to make an informed decision – which is allowed! – **Charley**

*In Conversation with...Rose Drew*

*How should a writer with a manuscript approach your press?*
Email is best, with a synopsis, a few comps, and the first few chapters; or two stories; or 10 poems (as appropriate). Don't worry about sending a very long letter, though do tell us about any significant previous important successes. Your work should speak for itself.
Also helpful are a few suggestions on how to attract readers: outreach ideas, links you have with media outlets or special interest groups.
If you know me personally, phone or text me.

*What does a standard author contract look like for you?*
We have an excellent contract, devised and okayed by a mid-level agent, and two literary solicitors. In a nutshell, we create the book, you okay any editorial changes, and we split profits. I will save more intricate details for private communications.

*What styles are you looking for? Are you open to cross-genre submissions?*
We love history, genre fiction (crime, sci-fi/fantasy, thriller), YA and children's lit, poetry, memoir, story collections, and 'cli-fi'. Some folks disparage that phrase but humans have less than a decade to make genuine changes to our wanton ways or human life is in peril. We've published cross-genre offerings: Don Walls' masterful play in verse, The Beggars of York, and story collections where the author included poems. Our anthologies often have artwork and photographs as well as stories and poetry.

*How do you judge the success of a book?*
If we must have several reprints; if the launch and promotional events create a buzz and are well attended; if readers tell us they love it – and buy more copies for friends and family; if we – the author and ourselves – feel delighted with how the experience has turned out. One true success is the

look on a new author's face when they hold their first book. I never tire of that.

*What's your favourite ever book?*
Too many to pick! Favourite of ours? They're all my babies! Of books I've read? My beloved authors include Abby Hoffman, Barbara Kingsolver, early Anne Tyler, Pat Conroy. "The Prince of Tides" by Conroy changed my life; helped me make peace with my difficult mother.
Often my favourite book is one we are working on most recently.

*How are authors expected to support marketing for their book?*
Stairwell Books features the very best writing from York and Yorkshire. We have offices in the US and UK, and distribute books to most countries. We hope authors will appear at launch and author events; promote their book – their piece of artwork – via word of mouth, social media. Reach out to institutions they have connections with: universities, libraries, local news outlets. Promote the book among their contacts, and locate the best venues in their own towns – they know the area best. Film a short segment reading and discussing their book.

*We asked Stairwell Books to select a title which represented their work:*

**The Water Bailiff's Daughter**
by Yvonne Hendrie

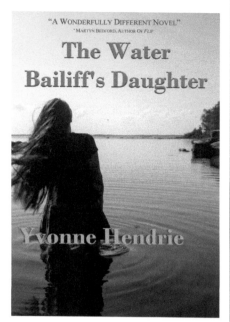

Helena Hailstanes is sick of the s
ecluded life her father Sam forces her
to live on the shores of Loch Duie.
Megan, as an angry young Sea Witch
cursed Helena and Sam, who are from
 an ancient race of shape-shifting
otters, to remain in human form.
With Megan in her life again, this
time meaning well, Helena embarks
on a course with the potential to harm
both herself and others.

*'A wonderfully different novella'* - Martyn Bedford.

*Contact details:*
Email Rose Drew or Alan Gillott: rose@stairwellbooks.com;
argillott@gmail.com
Twitter: @StairwellBooks
Website: www.stairwellbooks.co.uk

*How should a writer with a manuscript approach your press?*
For single-author works, authors should query the appropriate editor by sending a summary (max 400 words) and the first chapter OR 20 pages, whichever is longer. For multi-author works, including anthologies, send a brief proposal to the appropriate editor, outlining genre, potential contributors, length, etc.

*What does a standard author contract look like for you?*
We ask for non-exclusive rights to print paperbacks in English.

*What styles are you looking for? Are you open to cross-genre submissions?*
We publish fiction, poetry, and mixed anthologies, with a focus on books written or co-written between children and adults, and science fiction and fantasy.

*Contact details:*
Website: http://www.ellipsis.cx/~liana/ellipsisimprints/
Twitter: @EllipsisImprint

*In Conversation with...Janice Dempsey*

*How should a writer with a manuscript approach your Press?*
We only accept online submissions. Send us your finished, proofread sequence of poems in a Word (not a PDF) attachment, in a clear 12-point font (Arial, Times or Calibri). Don't format your manuscript more than you need to for the shape of your poems. (We'll set the margins, number the pages and add title pages, contents list, etc.) In your cover letter give your legal name, pen-name if you want to use one, postal address, phone number and a brief CV (150 words maximum)

*What does a standard author contract look like for you?*
Our author contract sets out mutual responsibilities including: our RRP policy; our promise to keep a title in print (for 5 years, currently); our reprint policy; authors' costs; commission we pay to authors when we sell their books online; our commitment to promote the book on social media, manage an individual author's page on our website and send out up to 5 review copies. Authors retain copyright on their poems.

*What styles are you looking for? Are you open to cross-genre submissions?*
We only publish poetry but within that we're open to all styles and genres. Recently we've published debut chap-books, retrospective collections and new collections by young and old, previously unpublished and established prize-winning poets; translations; humorous poems; autobiographical collections dealing with domestic abuse, adoption, chronic asthma and happier lives. Style doesn't concern us. We're looking for quality: original language and thought, 'heart', honesty and accessibility.

*How do you judge the success of a book?*
We judge our own books' successes by three measures: first, how proud we are to have been their publisher; secondly, have they attracted attention and sold the number of copies that we think it merits? Thirdly, have they attracted the attention of other good writers?

*What's your favourite ever book?*
From our own catalogue: "The Women Left Behind" by Imogen Russell Williams (2019). From the whole of literature: impossible to say, I love too many books equally, in a whole range of genres.

"Alice in Wonderland" and "Through the Looking Glass" were my earliest favourites and they remain near the top of my list for their wit, humour, absurdity and hidden depths.

*How are authors expected to support marketing for their book?*
Read at live and online events as often as possible, promote their books with accounts on Twitter, Facebook page and Instagram, and might use a signature on their email account with the book's title, its ISBN and a link to their author page on our site, as well as to their own website if they have one. They can encourage Amazon buyers to write reviews. They can send press releases to journals and local newspapers, inviting interviews and reviews.

*We asked Dempsey and Windle to select a title which represented their work:*

**The Women Left Behind**
by Imogen Russell Williams

Now and then writer and subject are perfectly matched. This is true of Imogen Russell Williams and her stranded women, drawn from mythology, drama and fiction. Each speaks out of her own situation: some bemused and seemingly helpless, some deeply distressed, some telling home truths about the shortcomings of men, some with a wonderful sense of the absurd, some exceedingly robust. Beautifully crafted, memorable poetry, illustrated with witty, elegant drawings by Chris Riddell.

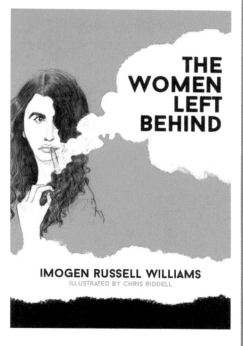

THE WOMEN LEFT BEHIND

IMOGEN RUSSELL WILLIAMS
ILLUSTRATED BY CHRIS RIDDELL

*Contact details:*
Janice Dempsey on Twitter: @DandWpublishing
Email: dempseyandwindle@gmail.com
Website: www.dempseyandwindle.com
Tel: 01483 571164 (landline preferred); mobile 07795660795
Postal address: 15 Rosetrees, Guildford, Surrey, GU1 2HS

# Maintaining your online presence
## post-publication

*"An online presence for an emerging writer can help aid sales and create a sense of trust with readers"*

Many authors believe that sourcing a traditional publisher for their manuscript will be the only marketing strategy that they need. Unfortunately, with much of today's marketing taking place online, and with so many books struggling for attention, marketing tends to be a collaborative process between publisher and author, particularly within the Small Press industry, where marketing budgets are often limited.

From the publisher's perspective, an author's presence online could impact the decision about manuscript acceptance. Many publishers will Google prospective author names to find out what social media they are interacting on, if any, if there are any performance videos or evidence of events attended online; if there is an author website. This helps a publisher gauge if there is an existing audience for the writer's work.

From the author's perspective, a presence online will help to reach readers and establish an audience from an angle which a publisher cannot create for the author: a personalised voice. Many surveys show that readers do take author personalities online into consideration when they are considering whether to buy a book. Therefore, an online presence for an emerging writer can help aid sales and create a sense of familiarity/trust with readers, which may be especially important for a debut.

When deciding how to present yourself online, it can be difficult to know what social media or online platforms will be most effective. If you live a busy lifestyle, I advise choosing just one account, to ensure you can be as engaged as possible. Twitter is a great place to start for writers, as it has a large #writingcommunity (following a hashtag may be one way to find fellow writers) who regularly share advice and celebrate successes. It may also be a fantastic opportunity to follow publisher accounts, read up on their latest books and witness the way they communicate online.

**– Isabelle**

*In Conversation with…Bernadette Jansen op de Haar*

*How should a writer with a manuscript approach your press?*
To submit a manuscript, authors should email us the complete text, preferably in Word format, together with a short covering email. We will acknowledge receipt and aim to make a decision within 4 to 6 weeks from submission. We accept manuscripts all year round directly from the author or through an agent. More details are available from
https://www.hollandparkpress.co.uk/about-us/submissions/

*What does a standard author contract look like for you?*
We offer our authors a royalty-based contract, standard percentage up to 2000 copies for fiction and 500 copies for poetry, and a higher rate for additional copies. The author receives free author copies and is entitled to purchase further copies at our author's discount for personal use and for resale.

*What styles are you looking for? Are you open to cross-genre submissions?*
We are looking for literary fiction and poetry. This includes novels, novellas, short story and full poetry collections. Literature is something we define as a work that the author had to write and which provides a compelling read to book buyers. We expect our authors to have their own unique voice and add something new and lasting to literature.

*How do you judge the success of a book?*
Our aim, of course, is to sell as many books as possible but, being realistic, we accept that not all titles achieve immediate success. So, that's why we think it is essential to give a book time to reach its potential, something which may well take several years. Good reviews and success in prizes are essential to create that crucial word of mouth but, ultimately, we want our books still being read many years from now.

*What's your favourite ever book?*
As the publisher, I get asked this question often and it's impossible to answer. I love many books but, for the books on our list, I actually invested my own money to get them published. I can't give higher praise. So, for this reason, I would like to nominate our entire list as my favourite book.

*How are authors expected to support marketing for their book?*
We expect our authors to be active on social media and be available for readings and interviews. With all the current live streaming techniques, geographical location is less of a limiting factor, though it is still in our contract. In short, we publish an author not just a book, so we work in partnership with our authors and are always open to develop and implement innovative promotional avenues.

*We asked Holland Park Press to select some titles which represent their work...*

**Upturned Earth**
by Karen Jennings

Upturned Earth by Karen Jennings is set in the copper mining district of the Cape Colony, 1886.

'Meticulously researched and grippingly told, this is an intensely human story that sheds light on a neglected corner of South African history' - Fiona Snyckers

ISBN 9781907320910

Upturned Earth
Karen Jennings

## A Sense of Tiptoe and other articles of faith
by Karen Hayes

A Sense of Tiptoe and other articles
of faith by Karen Hayes,
perceptive and lyrical poems
reflecting on the religious aspects
of faith and faith, or lack thereof,
in ourselves and our surroundings.

'engaging, illuminating and
entertaining' - The Pilgrim

ISBN 9781907320934

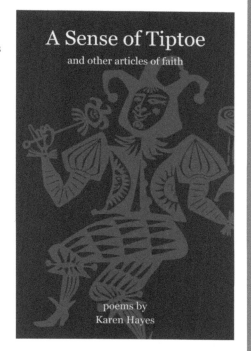

*Contact details:*
General email: enquiries@hollandparkpress.co.uk
Bernadette Jansen op de Haar, publisher: bernadette@hollandparkpress.
co.uk, + 44 (0) 7792611929
Website: https://www.hollandparkpress.co.uk/
Social Media:
https://www.hollandparkpress.co.uk/
https://twitter.com/HollandParkPres
https://www.facebook.com/HollandParkPress/
https://www.linkedin.com/company/holland-park-press/
https://www.pinterest.co.uk/bernadettejodh/boards/
https://www.instagram.com/hollandparkpress/
https://www.youtube.com/user/HollandParkPress/

*How should a writer with a manuscript approach your press?*
We're delighted to say that we're currently open for submissions. If you'd like to submit your work, we'd love to read it! In order to spare a few trees, we do ask that all submissions are sent via email — you can send the first few chapters, along with a completed cover letter, which can be downloaded from our website at renardpress.com/submissions.

*What does a standard author contract look like for you?*
We have a standard contract that we use, which covers everything you'd expect, and uses Society of Authors-approved royalty rates, as well as reasonable break and review clauses. We do not contractually oblige authors to be involved in marketing activities, but prefer to work with each individual author on a marketing and publicity plan.

*What styles are you looking for? Are you open to cross-genre submissions?*
We're currently considering both non-fiction and fiction with a literary bent; we aren't currently commissioning poetry, but look forward to doing so in the near future. We don't like to turn away submissions solely based on genre, however, and are essentially looking for 'good writing', in whatever form it may be!

*Contact details:*
You can contact us at: Renard Press Ltd, Kemp House, 152–160 City Road, London EC1V 2NX.
You can call us on 020 8050 2928, email us at info@renardpress.com, and you can also find us on Twitter @renardpress,
on Facebook @therenardpress, on Pinterest @renardpress and on Instagram @renardpress.

# PATRICIAN PRESS

*How should a writer with a manuscript approach your press?*
We prefer a personalised email rather than a generalised, multi-recipient one. Very often we are approached for agent representation, which seems rather inappropriate. Writers should give their reasons for writing to our press.

We prefer to receive the first three chapters of a novel and a synopsis or a selection of poems/short stories, rather than the whole work. We also like to see some biographical details about the writer.

*What does a standard author contract look like for you?*
Our author contract includes the standard publishing terms and conditions under UK law.
We don't however pay royalty advances. Royalties are based on receipts rather than a percentage of retail price as discounts vary enormously:

Paperback edition royalty: 25%
Digital edition: 50%
Permission fees: 50%

*What styles are you looking for? Are you open to cross-genre submissions?*
We normally publish fiction and poetry, but we will look at cross-genre. It is now sadly very difficult to classify a combination of fiction and non-fiction in one title, but we have published memoir.

*Contact details:*
Patrician Press, Manningtree.
Publisher: Patricia Borlenghi patricia@patricianpress.com
Co-publisher: Emma Kittle-Pey emma@patricianpress.com
Consultant editor: Anna Johnson anna@patricianpress.com

**VICTORINA PRESS**

*In Conversation with…Consuelo Rivera Fuentes*

*How should a writer with a manuscript approach your press?*
The writer should have good presentation of the manuscript, this is the first thing we see so it should make a good first impression. We look for professionalism and creativity. We ask for a clear structure to the story, and a plot synopsis of no longer than a page. This should be clear and concise. We also ask that the author has a basic knowledge of their audience and social media promotion to help us out with the marketing.

*What does a standard author contract look like for you?*
A standard author contract stipulates that, as the publisher, we have sole and exclusive right to produce and distribute the work. Our royalties sit at a standard 10% of net receipts and increase after 500 copies have been sold. The author gets 5 free copies and a discount in our shop. We take responsibility to publish the work at our own expense no later than 18 months after acceptance of the work. We publish the work in eBook format and offer royalties on these sales too. We also pay royalties on the net amounts received on any sales on subsidiary rights, ranging from 25-50%.

*What styles are you looking for? Are you open to cross-genre submissions?*
We are open to everything! We look primarily for quality, and we have no set restrictions. We currently publish historical fiction, children's fiction, hard-hitting prison memoirs, inspirational autobiographies, dystopian YA, vigilante fiction, literary fiction. Our books often cross genres and are difficult to box into categories. We publish bi-lingual anthologies and we have an academic book coming soon! Our mission is bibliodiversity, so anything that celebrates diverse voices will find a welcome home at Victorina.

*How do you judge the success of a book?*
Sales cannot be overlooked, but as an independent press focussed on bibliodiversity, we love to see a book improve representation in the market. We can't pretend we don't want to see high sales figures, but for us this is not the main aim. We want to celebrate all voices and have an impact on someone's life. We like to help other independent businesses, so if our books can help a small bookshop, this is a success!

*What's your favourite ever book?*
"Zami: A New Spelling of my Name" by Audre Lorde.

When I read Zami, I fell in love with the narrator, the author and her politics. Each reading teaches me how those elements change and evolve. Lorde's writing —passionate, powerful, personal, wise —gives me pleasure, strength and belief in myself when I feel alienated, an/other, in a culture whose racism is like a delicate, invisible scratch. Zami teaches me self-creation in relation, not isolation, always through a Lesbian lens and desire.

*How are authors expected to support marketing for their book?*
We want authors to have a website and a social media presence.
Social media is a huge marketing tool so promoting the book on Twitter, Facebook and Instagram can really get the book in front of people. We also like them to have a few writer or blogger friends that can help with reviews. A knowledge of their audience is invaluable as targeted marketing is the most effective.

*We asked Victorina Press to select a title which represented their work...*

**One Woman's Struggle in Iran: A prison Memoir**
by Nasrin Parvaz.

Award-winner in the Women's Issues category of the 2019 International Book Awards.

At 23, Parvaz was betrayed by a comrade in her fight for a non-Islamic state and arrested. For 8 years she faced torture, execution threats, starvation, and appalling living conditions. This is the story of her ordeal, her unbreakable spirit, of friendship, and of how women drew strength from one another.

*"Some books have to be written."*

*Contact details:*
Consuelos - consuelo.victorinapress@gmail.com
Jorge - jorge.victorinapress@gmail.com
Sophie - sophie.victorinapress@gmail.com

# *Author Marketing – Reviews and Interviews*

"Engage and offer to expand your publisher's reach where you can."

Public Relations can seem a daunting term, and certainly comes across as a time-consuming job! Small publishers will have varying departments when it comes to marketing. Typically, a larger team will assign roles in Public Relations (managing communications between the Press and the media, often organising events) and Marketing (anything budget related to books, such as advertising, social media, merchandise) separately. This is important for an author to understand because you will be working with these teams or individuals to help your book reach the largest audience possible.

As well as social media and an author website, an engaged publisher may suggest that you use your existing contacts within the writing community to gain reviews or interviews for your book. Authors come with their own contacts and these can be just as valuable as a publisher's pool of contacts. For example, you may know a friend with a popular book blog who you could ask for an interview, or you might be able to write a blog post for them about the process of writing your book. If you have time to assist your publisher in contacting local radio stations and newspapers, a collaborative approach to book marketing and gaining media/online attention can be truly effective. I always say to my marketing clients that book marketing only works on the 5th 'touch' – if a customer listens to your radio interview, reads a blog review, sees a social media graphic, watches a YouTube live reading and sees a local newspaper article, they will then be persuaded of the quality of your work enough to buy it!

Don't panic about being a marketing expert – that is the role of your publisher, and a large perk of traditional publishing – but do engage and offer to expand your publisher's reach where you can. It makes a huge difference! – **Isabelle**

*How should a writer with a manuscript approach your press?*
We ask that writers email through a full and complete manuscript to submissions@epoquepress.com. We ask for the full manuscript because if we like what we read we will want to keep on reading.

All submissions are assessed on literary merit alone and if authors wish to get a feel for what we particularly like then they need only have a read of the books we have published.

*What does a standard author contract look like for you?*
Our contracts our based around the author receiving a % royalty on each copy of the book sold and any associated rights sales.
We do not expect our authors to contribute anything financially to the production or marketing of the book.

*What styles are you looking for? Are you open to cross-genre submissions?*
We are very much focused on literary fiction which has a distinct and powerful voice. We are open for submissions of novels and collections of short stories. We are not looking for poetry, children's or YA novels as these are just not areas we know enough about.
We also run a regular é-zine in which we feature short stories, photography, visual art, spoken word, poetry, music and even short films.

*Contact details:*
General enquiries: Info@epoquepress.com

*In Conversation with... Louise Walters*

*How should a writer with a manuscript approach your press?*
I'm closed to submissions for a few months but will update my submissions page on my website when I'm open again: https://www.louisewalters-books.co.uk/submit

*What does a standard author contract look like for you?*
Like most other contracts...all the usual "stuff". I try to offer generous royalties to my authors, so those clauses may look a little different to Big 5 contracts.

*What styles are you looking for? Are you open to cross-genre submissions?*
I am looking for brilliant writing, first and foremost. I lean towards the literary, but I'm open to more or less any genre. I have a fondness for literary novellas. Long term, I would like to publish narrative non-fiction as well as fiction.

*How do you judge the success of a book?*
If money wasn't an issue, I would be pleased with lots of reviews and a wide readership for all my titles. However, money is an issue, so success is good sales. I work hard to achieve that, but it's very tough as an indie publisher to get my titles on enough radars.

*What's your favourite ever book?*
*Moon Tiger* by Penelope Lively. It could have been written for me. It's exactly my kind of novel.

*How are authors expected to support marketing for their book?*
I ask my authors to be as involved as possible. A strong social media presence is ideal. The ability to track down opportunities such as festivals, panels, signings... also a willingness to help me promote all my titles. I simply don't have the time to promote as much as I would like, nor the budget to market my books, so the more an author can do, the better.

*We asked Louise Walters Books to select a title which represented their work...*

**The Dig Street Festival**
by Chris Walsh
Out in April 2021.
It's an extraordinary novel: unique, original, funny, and moving. It's very much a Louise Walters Books book! Chris is a working-class writer, I'm a working-class publisher, and the novel is about working-class characters in working-class jobs. It explores male friendship and is surreal and bizarre as well as moving. Can't wait to publish this one!

*Contact details:*
I can be contacted via my website
https://www.louisewaltersbooks.co.uk/
Via email: info@louisewaltersbooks.co.uk
I can also be found on Twitter: @LouiseWalters12

VERVE POETRY PRESS

*In Conversation with...Stuart Bartholomew*

*How should a writer with a manuscript approach your press?*
We have a short submissions window each year, although what we are looking for might vary from one year to the next (i.e. pamphlets or full collections). We ask for complete or near complete manuscripts. Details for our next window can be found on our website. We also approach people we notice and value - getting to know us via a visit to Verve Poetry Festival, or on Twitter or Instagram, are good ways of starting this process.

*What does a standard author contract look like for you?*
Our royalties rise from 10% of book cover-price depending on whether the book sells via the book-trade or our website. Poets can purchase copies to sell at half-price but are under no obligation to.

Copyright for individual poems remains with the poet. We commit to keeping books in print in the contract, and to produce an eBook version. We don't insist on being brought your next book. We do ask you not to publish other books for a year on either side of publishing with us.

*What styles are you looking for? Are you open to cross-genre submissions?*
We are a poetry only press, although we are open to all forms of poetry from page to performance and everything between - poetry shows, long narrative, short lyrical, heavily edited, written in one go (and also creative non-fiction that has poetry links). But we like our poetry to be excellent, generous, colourful, open-minded, ambitious, meaningful and informed. The best way to understand what we like is to read some of our poets.

*How are authors expected to support marketing for their book?*
We look for poets who are willing to work hard to improve themselves as poets and to create reach for their poetry. We are committed to working hard for our books too, but as a small press with limited means, the support of our poets in getting their books out there is paramount. This might be via live events, online events, social media and other types of networking. Making the book has to be followed by showing the book, whatever form that takes.

*We asked Verve Poetry Press to select some titles which represented their work...'*

**Postcolonial Banter**
by Suhaiymah Manzoor-Khan

Postcolonial Banter is Suhaiymah Manzoor-Khan's debut collection. It features some of her best known and most widely performed poems as well as some never-seen-before material. Her words are a disruption of comfort, a call to action, a redistribution of knowledge and an outpouring of dissent. 'Suhaiymah's work is essential food for thought in these tumultuous times. Study it, think about it, make notes around it and treasure it because you are holding a piece of history in your hands.' - Lowkey.
**PBK**: £9.99 **ISBN**: 978 1 912565 24 5

**Eighty-Four**

Anthology curated by Helen Calcutt

Eighty-Four is an anthology of poetry on the subject of male suicide originally in aid of CALM (campaign against living miserably). Poems have been donated to the collection by Andrew McMillan, Salena Godden, Anthony Anaxagorou, Katrina Naomi, Ian Patterson, Carrie Etter, Peter Raynard, Caroline Smith and Joelle Taylor while a submissions window yielded many excellent poems on the subject from both known and hitherto unknown poets, we are thrilled to have been made aware of.

E ghty Four

Poems on male suicide, vulnerability, grief and hope.
Curated by Helen Calcutt.

Curated by poet Helen Calcutt, Eighty-Four showcases human vulnerability in all its forms. We hope to shed light on an issue that is cast in shadow, and often shrouded in secrecy and denial. If we don't talk, we don't heal, and we don't change. In Eighty-Four, we are talking. Are you listening?

**PBK**: £9.99  **ISBN:** 978 1 912565 13 9

*Contact details:*
https://vervepoetrypress.com
Twitter: @VervePoetryPres
Instagram: @verve.publisherofpoetry

*In Conversation with…Aisling Tempany*

*How should a writer with a manuscript approach your Press?*
Queries should be sent via email to editor@marblepoetry.com or by visiting the website. There is no specific format required, but submissions should consider that experimental works look quite different on a computer screen to a printed page or digital format and should consider this on submission.

*What does a standard author contract look like for you?*
A standard contract covers the responsibility the poet has to me, the legal obligation of Marble to publish the work, royalty rates and payment. Royalty rates are 15% net sales. Where possible, the author is expected to attend a launch event (once Covid 19 is through). If the author withdraws from an event without good reason, defined in the contract, they are expected to cover any costs incurred. I expect to have final decision on editing and changes. Covers are designed to be cohesive with Marble so although suggestions are welcome, I will make the final decision.

*What styles are you looking for? Are you open to cross-genre submissions?*
I am open on style but I would say I prefer modern perspectives and identities. I am open to cross genre submissions. I have found themed submissions to be the strongest for pamphlets. I consider a theme to be a specific place, person, or character, as is the case with Fordings and Red Queen, and Exile/Home. I am not keen on submissions which define the theme as 'loneliness' or 'relationships', which is too vague. I publish mini collections of up to 12 poems, large pamphlets up to 24 poems, and full-length collections of 48/50 poems. My favourite poets include Wislawa Szymborska, Anna Akhtamova, Marianne Moore.

*Contact details:*
Email: Editor@marblepoetry.com

# *Society of Authors Spotlight*

The Society of Authors (SoA) is an organisation that you may want to familiarise yourself with when you're looking to place your work. SoA is the UK trade union for a number of different creative families — including writers — and they offer several membership deals as well as a variety of services for a range of set fees.

Their website — www.societyofauthors.org — includes information on memberships, advisors (and how to seek help from them), and how to learn more about their funding opportunities, as they provide a number of grants and awards to aspiring and established authors throughout the year as well.

SoA is a good organisation for practical matters. They can provide advice on placing your book and, once an offer has been made, they offer services relating to publishing contracts and what you should be looking of/ staying mindful of. Liaising with the organisation provides security above all, but also easy access to services that might otherwise be hard to source (especially if you are just starting out in the creative writing industry).

The website — as listed above — is easily accessible and transparent in terms of what's being made available to members. A good starting point, then, might be to browse their Frequently Asked Questions to see for yourself whether it seems like a buyable service or, at least, keep them in mind for the future. **– Charley**

## ORENDA BOOKS

*In Conversation with... Karen Sullivan*

*How should a writer with a manuscript approach your press?*
We open for submissions several times a year, and writers will need to keep an eye on our website or social media for an alert. We'd like a full clean manuscript, covering letter with information about the author and a short pitch for the book, plus a full synopsis.

*What does a standard author contract look like for you?*
Our contracts are standard author contracts. We pay an advance and industry-standard royalty rates.

*What styles are you looking for? Are you open to cross-genre submissions?*
We publish literary fiction, with a heavy emphasis on crime thrillers (this year we won the CWA Crime & Mystery Publisher of the Year Award), but we love books that cross genre. The most important thing is the writing, and the originality of the work.

*How do you judge the success of a book?*
We don't have a 'set' criteria for judging the success of a book. We hope to achieve strong sales across all formats, but are also aware that it can take time to build an author and that the audience for a book can grow over a period of time, through word of mouth or post-publication marketing. We don't like to call any book 'back list'. Every book continues to receive our attention.

*What's your favourite ever book?*
I don't think I have one favourite! Books that have left a deep impression across the years include: *The Poisonwood Bible, Anne of Green Gables, A Visit from the Goon Squad, Sarah Gran's City of the Dead, Heart of Darkness, Fight Club, The Road*, anything by Margaret Atwood, Alice Munro or Carole Shields, *A Little Life* and most American Noir.

*How are authors expected to support marketing for their book?*
We expect authors to be as active on social media as they feel comfortable being…it's more important now than ever. Attend festivals (online and in person), support blog tours, share promotions and reviews of their books, take part in interviews as required, and become an engaged member of the book community.

*We asked Orenda Books to select a title which represented their work…*

When the body of a nineteen-year-old girl is found on the main street of Siglufjörður, Police Inspector Ari Thór battles a violent Icelandic storm in an increasingly dangerous hunt for her killer…
The chilling, claustrophobic finale to the international bestselling Dark Iceland series.

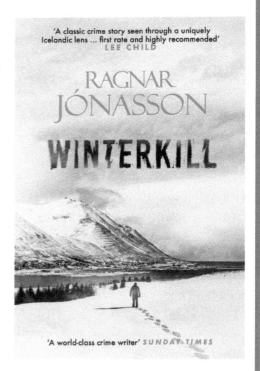

'A classic crime story seen through a uniquely Icelandic lens … first rate and highly recommended'
LEE CHILD

RAGNAR JÓNASSON

WINTERKILL

'A world-class crime writer' SUNDAY TIMES

*Contact details:*
Email: info@orendabooks.co.uk
Twitter: @OrendaBooks
Instagram: @orendabooks

*How should a writer with a manuscript approach your press?*
They should start by reading our submissions page to see if they feel their writing would be a good fit for us, and if we would be a good fit for their writing. If they are happy that might be the case, they should then email us with a synopsis and either the first 5,000 words or the first three chapters.

*What does a standard author contract look like for you?*
A standard author contract is one that outlines the proposed agreement between the parties involved in a clear and concise way. It shows clearly the obligations, including the costs and benefits to all, with no room for ambiguity.

*What styles are you looking for? Are you open to cross-genre submissions?*
Our overriding aim is to publish the books people want to read, within the broad genres of crime, thriller and suspense. We judge each submission on its own merit, without thought as to exactly what genre it fits into. It is rare that one size fits all.

*Contact details:*
Rebecca Collins and Adrian Hobart: hobeckbooks@gmail.com

*How should a writer with a manuscript approach your press?*
Look out for our open book submission windows on our website (404ink.
com/submissions) which open once or twice a year. We ask for an
explanation of why 404 Ink is a good fit for your book, the first 30
pages of the manuscript, and a 150-word bio. Our new non-fiction
Inklings strand, for big ideas in a small format, is open for submissions
year-round.

*What does a standard author contract look like for you?*
We of course prefer to obtain World rights but often accept UK &
Commonwealth rights. We try our best to start royalties at around 15%
and always produce print and eBook editions. Details are worked out upon
offer.

*What styles are you looking for? Are you open to cross-genre
submissions?*
We are open to contemporary fiction, cross-genre, unusual, dark,
challenging fiction, humour, short stories, underrepresented voices, and
also currently relevant cultural/social issue non-fiction in particular. We
also have our pocket-sized non-fiction series Inklings, presenting big ideas in
a small format, which takes on a range of cultural, educational and societal
subjects.

*Contact details:*
Website: 404ink.com
Email: hello@404ink.com
Twitter: @404Ink

*In Conversation with... Jenn Thompson*

*How should a writer with a manuscript approach your press?*
We announce submission windows on our social media channels and in our newsletter. Outside of our official submission windows, you can contact us via the Contact Us page on our website to tell us a bit more about yourself and your book. If we're interested, we'll ask to read a sample.

*What does a standard author contract look like for you?*
We pay an advance against royalties, and then royalties on copies sold. We will negotiate territory and subsidiary rights on a book-by-book basis.

*What styles are you looking for? Are you open to cross-genre submissions?*
We publish adult fiction and creative non-fiction by queer-identified authors. We're open to any style and genre as long as it sits somewhere within the literary bracket and reflects some aspect of the queer experience. We are open to cross-genre submissions.

*How do you judge the success of a book?*
We'd consider a book successful if it reaches its readers and if it's available widely in retailers, if it's well reviewed, if the author is happy with its launch into the world. We're a queer press first and foremost and we consider our books successful if they are enjoyed by queer readers, if they are helpful in some way.

*What's your favourite ever book?*
That's an incredibly hard question! There are so many favourites. But a recent favourite that sums up what we want to achieve with Cipher Press is "Paul Takes the Form of a Mortal Girl" by Andrea Lawlor - a dirty, smart, loveable book that's quintessentially queer.

*How are authors expected to support marketing for their book?*
We like to work closely with our authors and will talk about marketing early on. We expect all our authors to be available for some kind of marketing and publicity support, but also understand not everyone is comfortable doing live events, face-to-face interviews etc. We find out what our authors are happy with and build a plan around that - whether it will be mostly online or live.

*We asked Cipher Press to select a title which represented their work...*

Transgressive, foulmouthed, and wildly funny, 100 Boyfriends is a filthy, unforgettable, and brutally profound ode to messy queer love. From one-night stands to recurring lovers, Brontez Purnell's characters expose themselves to racist neighbours, date Satanists, and drink their way out of trouble, all the while fighting the urge to self-sabotage. Drawing us into a community of glorious misfits living on the margins of a white supremacist, heteronormative society, Purnell gives us an uncompromising vision of desire, desperation, race, loneliness, and queerness.

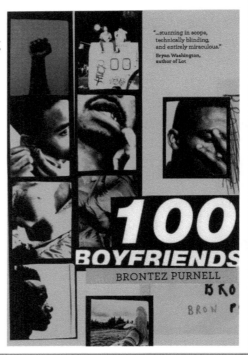

*Contact details:*
Jenn Thompson: jenn@cipherpress.co.uk
Ellis K: ellis@cipherpress.co.uk

## In Conversation with...Helen Lewis

*How should a writer with a manuscript approach your press?*
We are open to unsolicited and agented manuscripts. You can read our full submission guidelines here:
https://www.hashtagpress.co.uk/submissionguidelines
We read every email that comes in. We review submissions via email and occasionally host in-person and virtual pitch sessions.
We only review submissions via email.
Please email submissions@hashtagpress.co.uk.
For Children, middle-grade, YA, Chick-lit books: In subject heading address it to Abiola Bello.
Non-fiction, Psychological Thrillers, Crime fiction, Women's fiction books: In subject heading address it to Helen Lewis.
See also: Hashtag BLAK, our new Imprint.

*What does a standard author contract look like for you?*
Hashtag Press and our imprint, Hashtag BLAK, operate as a traditional publishing house. We are focused on supporting talented writers with the best production, PR, marketing and sales values possible for a small but perfectly formed, female-led, indie publishing house like ours! Our contracts are pretty standard to be honest, no upfront costs expected from the author (although we do expect our authors to work hard, collaborate and contribute in terms of their time and energy). We are renowned for our strong social media and PR campaigns.

*What styles are you looking for? Are you open to cross-genre submissions?*
We love diverse and inclusive books, own voices stories, and more than anything we just want to read really good submissions by authors who know their art and are passionate and hard-working.

*Contact details:*
Website: www.hashtagpress.co.uk
Email: submissions@hashtagpress.co.uk
Twitter: @Hashtag_press

*In Conversation with...Nathan Evans*

*How should a writer with a manuscript approach your press?*
We're a very small press - just two of us - so, as much as we'd love to, we're not able to read manuscripts year-round. We announce submission windows on our website and socials.

*What does a standard author contract look like for you?*
We are fair and transparent with our authors: author percentages on paperbacks are 10% RRP, on eBooks 50% net. We like to have world-wide English language rights as we publish through Kindle Paperback in non-UK markets. We like to have Audio book rights and also translation and dramatic rights for a time-limited period.

*What styles are you looking for? Are you open to cross-genre submissions?*
We are interested in writers underrepresented in mainstream publishing, specifically BAME, LGBTQ+ and working-class writers. Generally, we publish literary fiction, but also poetry, non-fiction and books with a photographic element.

*Contact details:*
nathan@inkandescent.co.uk

*In Conversation with…Farhaana Arefin and Brekhna Aftab*

*How should a writer with a manuscript approach your press?*
As a nascent publisher with limited resources, we will have a short period each year to receive submissions for the following year's list. Before this window opens, we'll share our guidelines for submitting proposals. We ask authors to list the writers and works that inspire them, instead of a list of competing works. If an idea moves us and we want to take it forward, we'll develop the proposal with you!

*What does a standard author contract look like for you?*
We've tried to embed our community-building ethos and collaborative spirit in every aspect of our publishing model, including author contracts. Whether signing first-time or established authors, we pay advances on principle. We want authors to share in each other's success, so we pay a higher royalty rate on sales through Hajar subscriptions, while also paying fair escalating rates on individual copy sales. We seek author approval on cover design and try to match trade subsidiary royalties as an indie.

*What styles are you looking for? Are you open to cross-genre submissions?*
Cross-genre submissions are our bread and butter. We publish fiction, nonfiction and everything in between: oral histories, autofiction, poetry, essays. The backbone of our list is political engagement; this can be through the articulation of how political structures shape our lives, and/or through the political choice to use the page as a place of unfettered creative expression and liberation. Our raison d'être is to provide writers of colour with a space to experiment, push boundaries and create new worlds.

*Contact details:*
Hajar Press's publishers are Brekhna Aftab and Farhaana Arefin.
We can be reached at www.hajarpress.com/contact and on social media at
@hajarpress.

# ONWE PRESS

*How should a writer with a manuscript approach your press?*
We accept submissions of completed manuscripts via submissions@onwe-press.com. Best practices would be to include a short synopsis of the book, a full detailed summary and at least 10 chapters of the manuscript for us to review.

*What does a standard author contract look like for you?*
We're really keen to see authors earn out of their advances early, so we offer a smaller advance in exchange for substantially higher royalties. We have a team dedicated to ensuring that creatives get paid their due for their world-changing work and the principal way that we ensure this is by giving authors a larger share of the royalty pie.

*What styles are you looking for? Are you open to cross-genre submissions?*
We accept all genres and books of all styles, shapes, and sizes. We publish trade books for a general audience, from fiction to nonfiction, across varying age groups.

The only restrictions that we currently have in place are with the story itself. At Onwe, it's important that our books tell a different narrative. So we are looking for unique stories from diverse voices and/or stories that centre under-represented ideals, characters, and cultures.

*Contact details:*
To submit a manuscript for review, email submissions@onwepress.com. For general enquiries, contact us at info@onwepress.com. You can also keep up to date with Onwe on Twitter and Instagram using the handle @weareonwe. We look forward to hearing from you!

*How should a writer with a manuscript approach your press?*
Our submission guidelines are clear on our website. Writers should consider whether their work fits our press, preferably by checking out our books in advance (although this is not a requirement for submission). We get sent a lot of inappropriate work, so taking time to check us out will endear you to us.

*What does a standard author contract look like for you?*
We don't pay an advance, but we split profits 50/50 with every author. As we've made profits on all of our books, we think this is a fair deal.

*What styles are you looking for? Are you open to cross-genre submissions?*
We are open to all sorts of literary fiction and poetry. The more cross-genre the better!

*Contact details:*
Editor, Sophie Essex. Email: editorsalopress@gmail.com.
Website: www.salopress.com

*In Conversation with... Haley Jenkins*

*How should a writer with a manuscript approach your press?*
With knowledge, integrity and personality. I like to see the writer has made an effort in their cover email without the words 'emerging', 'prize-winning' or similar 'buzz words'. I want to see that they have read our work, even if it is our free blog publications. I often see a generic email from someone who has obviously sent it to many publishers at once. Harsh but true advice: if you want someone to make the effort to read your work, make the effort to sell it to them.

*What does a standard author contract look like for you?*
We generally don't have a contract as such. I lay everything out on the Submission Guidelines and go over it again in greater detail when we accept work. But everything is there for them to read before they even submit. Every writer should retain the rights to their work, we involve them 100% of the way from the editing process to the book cover design to the marketing. We ensure the author has a good experience with us and we form a good relationship.

*What styles are you looking for? Are you open to cross-genre submissions?*
We are totally open for cross-genre submissions! We aren't too prescriptive over style, we enjoy work that is a little odd, a little off the mainstream road, we love strong characters and unusual poetry with strong, evocative language use. We're passionate about the raw, the real and the weird. We accept poetry, fiction, memoir, interviews, reviews, non-fiction, CNF and more!

*Contact details:*
contact@selcouthstation.com
Twitter: @selcouthstation
Instagram: @selcouthstation
Facebook: Selcouth Station Press

# About the Editors

**Isabelle Kenyon** is a northern writer and the author of chapbooks: This is not a Spectacle, Digging Holes To Another Continent (Clare Songbirds Publishing House, New York, 2018), Potential (Ghost City Press, 2019), Growing Pains (Indigo Dreams Publishing Ltd, 2020) and one short story with Wild Pressed Books (Short Story 'The Town Talks', 2020). She is the editor of Fly on the Wall Press, a socially conscious small press for chapbooks and anthologies. She has had poems and articles published internationally in journals such as Ink, Sweat and Tears and newspapers such as The Somerville Times and The Bookseller.

She was listed in the Streetcake Experimental Writing Prize 2020; 2019 and for The Word, Lichfield Cathedral Competition 2019. Her poems have been published in poetry anthologies by Indigo Dreams Publishing, Verve Poetry Press, and Hedgehog Poetry Press. She has performed at Cheltenham Poetry Festival and Verbose, Manchester in 2020, Leeds International Festival as part of the 'Sex Tapes', Apples and Snakes' 'Deranged Poetesses' in 2019 and Coventry Cathedral's Plum Line Festival in 2018. She is a fierce dog lover and a confessed caffeine addict.

**Dr Charley Barnes** is an academic and author from the West Midlands, UK. She is the author of several poetry publications, including: A Z-hearted Guide to Heartache (V. Press, 2018); Body Talk (Picaroon Poetry, 2019); Hierarchy of Needs: A Retelling, co-authored with Claire Walker (V. Press, 2020), and Lore: Flowers, Folklore, and Footnotes (Black Pear Press, 2021). Charley has also authored three short fiction releases: Death Is A Terrible House Guest (The Black Light Engine Room Press, 2019); Burn The Witch (The Black Light Engine Room Press, 2020) and Go On A Road Trip (Wild Press Books, 2020). Under Charlotte Barnes, Charley writes crime fiction, including the titles: Intention; The Copycat; The Watcher; and The Cutter (Bloodhound Books, 2019-2021). She has had individual poems and fiction pieces published by the likes of Ink, Sweat and Tears, Riggwelter Press, and Bind Collective.

Charley is the current Managing Director of Sabotage Reviews, the editor of Dear Reader, and a lecturer in Creative and Professional Writing at the University of Wolverhampton. She has spoken and performed at events such as Verve Poetry Festival, Cheltenham Poetry Festival, and Tamworth Literature Festival, where she formed part of a panel to discuss the practicalities of publishing crime for a contemporary readership. Charley was the Worcestershire Poet Laureate 2019-2020. She is now the Writer-in-Residence for The Swan Theatre, Worcester, and their associated venues. When she isn't writing, she's likely drinking tea, eating cake, or walking her dog.

# RESOURCES

**Places Isabelle Kenyon likes to go to for further submission opportunities...**

New Writing North newsletter
Writing East Midlands newsletter
Authors Publish (a newsletter and a website)
Angela Carr's monthly roundup: https://angelatcarr.wordpress.com/

**Places Dr. Charley Barnes likes to go to for further submission opportunities...**

National Associate of Writers in Education website
Writing West Midlands website
The Poets Directory website

## About Fly on the Wall Press

A publisher with a conscience.
Publishing high quality stories, poetry and anthologies on pressing issues, from exceptional writers around the globe. Founded in 2018 by founding editor, Isabelle Kenyon.

## Other publications:
*Please Hear What I'm Not Saying*
*Persona Non Grata*
*Bad Mommy / Stay Mommy* by Elisabeth Horan
*The Woman With An Owl Tattoo* by Anne Walsh Donnelly
*the sea refuses no river* by Bethany Rivers
*White Light White Peak* by Simon Corble
*Second Life* by Karl Tearney
*The Dogs of Humanity* by Colin Dardis
*Small Press Publishing: The Dos and Don'ts* by Isabelle Kenyon
*Alcoholic Betty* by Elisabeth Horan
*Awakening* by Sam Love
*Grenade Genie* by Tom McColl
*House of Weeds* by Amy Kean and Jack Wallington
*No Home In This World* by Kevin Crowe
*The Goddess of Macau* by Graeme Hall
*The Prettyboys of Gangster Town* by Martin Grey
*The Sound of the Earth Singing to Herself* by Ricky Ray
*Inherent* by Lucia Orellana Damacela
*Medusa Retold* by Sarah Wallis
*Pigskin* by David Hartley
*We Are All Somebody*
*Someone Is Missing Me* by Tina Tamsho-Thomas
*Aftereffects* by Jiye Lee

## Social Media:
@fly_press (Twitter)
@flyonthewall_poetry (Instagram)
@flyonthewallpress (Facebook)
www.flyonthewallpress.co.uk

Lightning Source UK Ltd.
Milton Keynes UK
UKHW051438060821
388251UK00010B/21